KT-368-889

# History of Costume

## Tim Healey

DORNOCH ACADEMY

——::——

CLASS **PRIZE**

AWARDED TO

ANGELA MORRISON

CLASS SII

FOR

ATTAINMENT

Rector

25-6-81

## Macdonald Educational

# Contents

**How to use this book**
First look at the contents page and see if the subject you are looking for is listed. For instance if you want to find out about shops, you will see that **Shops** are on page 26. The index will tell you how many times a particular subject is listed. For instance, you will see that shops are also listed on pages 27, 42.

page

6 **Why clothes?**
Why people wear clothes. Magic. Learning how to make clothes. Materials used for making clothes.

8 **Look at me**
How clothes attract. Why a fashion starts. How fashions change over the years.

10 **Clothes and society**
Laws about wearing clothes. How clothes show what a person does.

12 **Spinning and weaving**
Spinning, weaving and printing materials. Ways of making clothes. Clothes in Egypt and central Asia.

14 **The ancient world**
How the Cretans, Greeks and Romans dressed.

16 **The Dark Ages**
The fall of the Roman Empire. Tribes begin to move all over Europe taking their different customs and clothes with them. Byzantine dress.

18 **The Middle Ages**
Clothes become more fitting. The effect of the Crusades on fashion.

20 **The tailor's art**
Padding and slashing make clothes more elaborate. Women begin to wear hoops and corsets. The extravagance of court dress. What people wore in the country.

22 **Puritans and Cavaliers**
Civil war splits England, the two sides wear very different clothes. The fashion for wigs. The jacket comes into being.

24 **Ladies and gentlemen**
How men and women dressed in the eighteenth century. The French Revolution. The Macaroni club.

**26 Buying and selling**
Village markets. Buying and selling in the towns. What the shops were like.

**28 The machine age**
The invention of machines speeds up the making of materials. Poor people and their clothes.

**30 Working clothes**
Trousers and the three-piece suit. Regional and peasant costume.

**32 Clothes for women**
The classical style. The return of corsets and full skirts. Crinolines and bustles. Rational clothes.

**34 New freedoms**
Flappers. How sports affected clothes. World War II and 'making do'.

**36 The great fashion houses**
Fashion dolls and fashion plates.

The growth of a fashion industry. How designers work. Fashion sensations. The New Look and the mini skirt.

**38 Young fashions**
Clothes for young people. Changes in men's hairstyles. The effect of entertainment on fashions. Styles from abroad.

**40 Protective clothes**
Armour and aprons. The protective clothes that we wear now. Rainwear and mackintoshes.

**42 Making clothes today**
Department stores and boutiques. Self-service shops and shopping centres. New materials for making clothes.

**44 More books to read and places to visit**

**45 Index**

# Why clothes?

Human beings are the only creatures that wear clothes. Some of us cover ourselves from head to foot. How many pieces of clothing are you wearing? You may be wearing more than ten.

We can only guess why people started to wear clothes. It may have been to protect themselves against the weather. Yet human skin has a layer of fat underneath it. The fat gives good protection against heat and cold. Think of your face. Even on a cold day, you do not cover it up. The face adapts to changes in the weather.

Primitive people often wear few clothes even in cold climates. Their bodies adapt just as our faces do. We need clothes less than you might think.

This cave painting shows a deer. The hunters used the deer that they killed for many things.

## Magic

People may have begun to wear clothes for magical protection. They painted their skins and scarred themselves in patterns to keep away evil spirits. They thought the patterns would bring them good luck. They wore charms made from bears' and sharks' teeth, reindeer antlers and snakes' skins. They believed that the strength of these fierce creatures would then pass into their own bodies.

## Skins

People used to wear the skins of animals they had killed. The skins were warm. In cold climates, people began to wear them more often. The skins were stiff and scratchy. People learnt how to soften them. They also learnt how to sew the skins together using animal sinew or vegetable fibre for thread. They made needles from the bones of fish and animals. They may even have made buttons from animal bones.

They made buttons from the bones.

## Other materials

Later people learnt how to spin and weave cloth. In cold climates they used the wool from animals they raised to make cloth. In warmer climates they made lighter clothes from flax and cotton. The ancient Chinese learnt to make silken cloth over 4,500 years ago.

Different clothes came from different needs. In cold lands people liked to wear thick trousers to keep their legs warm. But in hot lands, people just draped cloth around themselves in different ways.

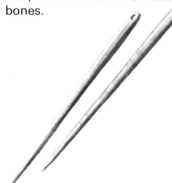

They could make needles to sew with from the bones too.

The primitive Indian tribes
that live in Brazil paint
their bodies with spots.
They believe that if they
copy the spots of the
leopard they will gain its
strength and courage.

# Look at me

comb

powder and
paint pots

mirror

tweezers

Birds and animals do not wear clothes. But many animals put on a special display when they want to attract a mate. People 'dress up' to attract attention. We use clothes and jewellery for display. When we dress up for a party we are using our clothes just as a peacock uses his tail.

## Fashion

Fashions were started by royalty and nobility. They wore beautiful silks and costly jewellery to show off their rank and power. Now it is the fashion designers who set the new styles. If people like the designs they are copied all over the world. When everybody wears this style it stops being surprising and becomes old-fashioned. The designers think up new ideas and fashions change again.

Fashions used to last much longer than they do now, but even in 1380 a writer complained: 'To be a good tailor yesterday is no good today. Cut and fashions change too quickly'.

## Fashion variations

There have been many fashions over the past centuries. They were all thought very beautiful at the time.

Throughout the ages people have tried to make themselves look attractive.

Above left: Venetian women of the sixteenth century wore 'zoccolos' to keep their skirts from dragging in the mud.

Above right: Elizabethan dandies wore their finery for the same reason that a peacock spreads its tail— they wanted to be attractive to other people.

Left: These are some of the things that an Egyptian woman would have used to put on her make-up. Her face might have been made-up like the bottom picture.

In China until early in this century, some wealthy women had their feet tightly bound to stop them growing. Tiny feet were thought very elegant, although it was very difficult to walk.

Narrow waists for both men and women have been admired for centuries. People used to wear very tight corsets. Wide skirts make the waist look smaller. Fashionable women wore skirts so wide that they had to be held out with hoops.

Legs have often attracted attention. In the eighteenth century men wore false calves if their legs were skinny. When fashionable women first wore short skirts in the 1920's they were thought very shocking. The mini-skirts of the 1960's also caused a great stir.

People will put up with a lot of discomfort and danger to be fashionable. Some early make-up was bad for the complexion and even poisonous. Ladies could not bend in tight corsets. The corsets caused diseases of the lungs and pushed the ribs out of place. Ladies wore them, all the same.

9

# Clothes and society

Today there are no laws about wearing fine clothes. Until recently the rich and the noble set the fashions.

Before the eighteenth century there were laws to stop merchants and the poorer people from looking too smart. These were called 'sumptuary' laws.

In the Middle Ages fashionable men wore long pointed shoes. A sumptuary law said that noblemen could wear them more than 60 cms beyond the toe. Gentlemen could wear them up to 30 cms and commoners could wear them only 15 cms beyond the toe. The law made sure that the nobles stood out most!

Above: Sometimes young people dress in clothes that are very alike. It is almost like wearing a uniform.

## Clothes to show rank

Some people wear clothes that show that they have a specially important place in society. Kings and queens wear royal costume for state occasions. Churchmen wear ceremonial robes. Mayors wear heavy chains of office. These clothes make the wearers seem grander than everyone else. They have been worn for many centuries. They are now quite out of date. Their aim is to make us respect old customs and traditions.

In the eighteenth century men shaved their heads and wore wigs. The custom died out long ago, but judges in England still wear wigs to make them seem important.

Right: Some people wear uniforms to show what jobs they do. It is easy to recognize traffic wardens, nurses and policemen by the clothes they wear.

## Clothes to show jobs

In some jobs it is useful for the worker to stand out in a crowd. Nurses and air hostesses, for example, wear uniform so that people can recognize them if they need help. Team colours in sports are a kind of uniform. A footballer must be able to tell at a glance which side a player is on.

Uniforms also show that a person has special powers that an ordinary person does not have. We can recognize a traffic warden instantly by his or her uniform. We know that a traffic warden can give 'tickets' for parking offences. In the same way we can see a policeman in his uniform and know that he has a job with special powers. How many other uniforms can you think of?

In a shop we can tell which people are shop assistants by the clothes that they wear. We know which people to ask to help us. Uniforms make a person stand out.

In the Middle Ages it was fashionable to extend the toes of men's shoes far beyond their toes. The length of the points on the shoes showed the man's status, the longer they were the more important the man was. When the weather was wet they wore wooden pattens under the shoes to keep them dry.

At many times over the years clothes have become very exaggerated. This cartoon is poking fun at the fashion for very tightly laced waists.

# Spinning and weaving

People learnt to make thread thousands of years ago. Raw wool or flax was fixed onto a weight called a spindle. The spindle was set spinning and gradually fed out the raw wool or flax. It twisted into long thin strands which wound around the bottom of the spindle.

Two sets of thread were used to make cloth. The first set was held in place on a loom. It was called the warp thread. The second thread was passed alternately over and under the warp threads. It was called the weft thread. The weavers pushed the rows of weft thread together. This made cloth.

Sometimes people dyed the threads in different colours and then wove them on the loom. This made patterned cloth. They also stitched patterns on to the cloth after it had been woven. This is called embroidery. Designs were printed on to plain cloth with carved wooden, or clay, stamps.

These early ways of making and decorating cloth have hardly changed for thousands of years.

## Draping and stitching

There were two main ways of wearing cloth. The simplest way was to drape it around the body and hold it in place with a knot or a brooch. Kilts and capes were worn in this way. The other way was to cut and stitch the material. Clothes like dresses and trousers that fit closely over the body, arms and legs are made like this.

## Ancient Egypt

The clothes in ancient Egypt were made of draped white linen. The men wore a loincloth wrapped around their hips. Women wore narrow dresses held up over the shoulders. They wore draped dresses with long sleeves.

## Central Asia

The people from the ancient civilizations of central Asia were originally mountain dwellers. As they lived in a cold climate, they wore warmer, more fitted clothes. They rode horses and needed specially cut clothes. Their clothes were made of leather, silk and wool. The men wore sleeved tunics and breeches that reached to the knees or ankles. Women wore robes, sometimes with long wide sleeves.

This Greek woman is wearing draped clothes. The material is not sewn at all.

Persian people wore clothes that were sewn to a more tailored shape.

These are the tools that people have used to make cloth. Some are still used today and have remained unchanged for many hundreds of years.

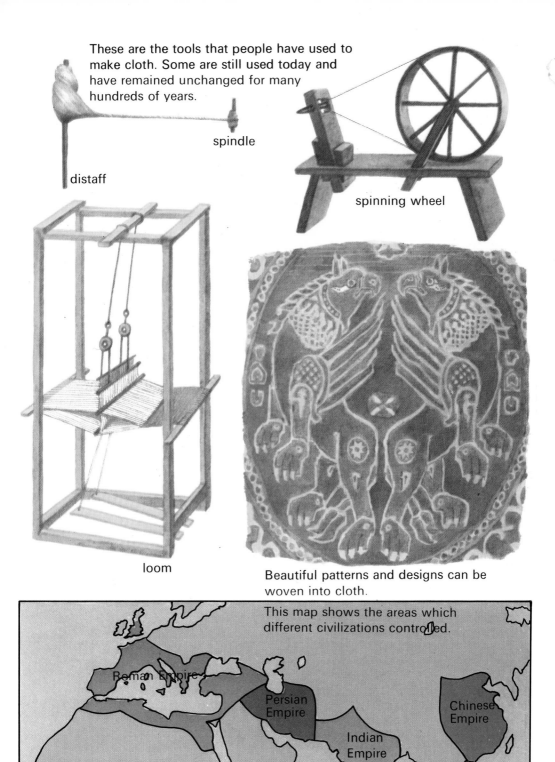

spindle

distaff

spinning wheel

loom

Beautiful patterns and designs can be woven into cloth.

This map shows the areas which different civilizations controlled.

Roman Empire

Persian Empire

Chinese Empire

Indian Empire

Indo-China

# The ancient world

While the great Egyptian civilization still flourished on the River Nile new civilizations grew up in Europe. One of these was on the island of Crete. The Cretans were a gay, sports loving people. Their clothes had bright patterns and were shaped in new ways. Cretan women sometimes wore long full skirts that were tight around the waist. They wore short embroidered jackets on top. Cretan men liked to show off their waists too. They wore wide, tight belts.

## Greek dress

The Greeks, like the ancient Egyptians, wore clothing of draped linen. The basic garment was a tunic or 'chiton'. Men wore them short to the knee. Women wore them pinned at the shoulders and reaching to the ground. They were tied around the waist with a cord and hung in graceful folds. Over the chiton, women wore another draped robe called a 'peplos'. In cold weather large cloaks called 'himations' were worn.

This man is wearing a traditional Roman toga. It is draped over his body.

Left: Two different kinds of tunic were worn in Greece. The man is wearing a short Doric tunic with a cloak. The woman is wearing a long Ionic tunic with a cloak called a himation over it.

Right: These are some of the hairstyles that women wore at the time of the Roman Empire.

Far right: In Crete small waists were very much admired. Cretans also liked brightly patterned material.

## Roman dress

The Romans wore draped clothes too. They were made of wool, linen, silk and leather. Both men and women wore short tunics. Men covered theirs with carefully draped cloaks called 'togas'. Women wore sleeved robes called 'stolas'. The togas were very full and could not be worn for active work. They were worn only by wealthy and important Romans. Only high officials were allowed to wear togas with purple borders, and the Emperor wore a toga dyed all over purple. The dye was very expensive to make and was reserved only for this special use.

The Romans had a vast empire and occupied lands as far apart as North Africa and England. Their clothes were copied in many of these lands.

Many of the tribesmen in the conquered lands wore trousers. The Romans thought that these were undignified. They even made laws to stop Roman men wearing trousers. Some Roman soldiers who guarded the chilly north frontiers of the Empire wore them all the same.

Poor Romans did not wear a toga. They wore a short tunic and in cold weather a cloak or paenula.

# The Dark Ages

The Romans called the people that lived around the borders of their Empire 'barbarians'. Many of the barbarians could not read or write. They did not know how to build fine cities and beautiful homes. When the power of Rome began to break down, the barbarians destroyed many Roman cities and settled there themselves. The Huns came into Italy from the East. They had come from Mongolia. Their clothes were rough and primitive. They wore coarse leather trousers and tunics of cloth woven from camel or yak hair. They had fur cloaks. Their arms and legs were often bare.

Tribes of Goths and Teutons attacked the Empire from the north of Europe. At first, these Northern barbarians wore clothes of leather and hide. Later they learnt to make clothes of wool, felt and linen. Some of their clothes have been found preserved for hundreds of years in peat bogs.

Northern tribesmen wore tunics, breeches and cloaks. The cloaks were thick and could be used for blankets. Some were woven in plaid designs. The women wore long skirts held up with buckled belts or girdles. Sometimes they wore two belts. They hung decorations on the second.

When the Romans left Britain in about AD 450 the country was invaded by Angles, Jutes and Saxons. They wore various kinds of tunics and breeches with cloaks. Women wore long tunics and over-dresses. Beautiful metal work from these times—brooches, shields, helmets and clasps—can be seen in many museums.

## Byzantine dress

By the fourth century the power of the Roman Empire had collapsed. The Roman Emperor Constantine, who was a Christian, moved his capital to the city of Byzantium. Here Eastern influence was strong. The draped Roman styles gave way to more fitted clothes. Noble men and women wore long-sleeved shirts reaching to the ground. They wore magnificent cloaks. They learned how to weave silk from the Chinese and the Persians. They wore brightly coloured fabrics with designs of magical creatures. They used gold and silver threads and sewed pearls and jewels onto their clothes.

The clothes that the Huns wore were usually made of fur and leather.

The jewellery made in Anglo-Saxon England was very beautiful.

history of Costume !
...somy — nothing on
national costume)

(13 +14 yrs)

ANGELA

MORRISON

Clothes in Byzantium were very richly decorated. Precious jewels were often sewn onto them, or they were heavily embroidered.

The clothes that the Anglo-Saxons wore were much plainer. They were made from materials like wool and linen.

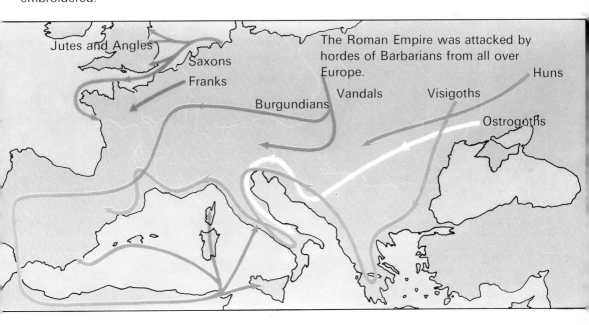

Jutes and Angles

Saxons

Franks

Burgundians

The Roman Empire was attacked by hordes of Barbarians from all over Europe.

Vandals

Visigoths

Huns

Ostrogoths

# The Middle Ages

Veil and wimple

Fillet and barbette worn on top of a crispine

Fillet and veil

In the Middle Ages married women nearly always covered their hair. They wore head-dresses like these.

In the Middle Ages most people worked on the land. Everyone, except the very wealthy, made their own clothes. Local materials were used, such as wool, linen and leather. Dyes were made from plants such as lichens, onions and alder. Earths were used too. Nobles wore silks which had been sent from Turkey and Italy.

The shape of the tunic was still quite simple, but it fitted the body more closely. Cloaks and well-fitting stockings or 'hose' were worn too. Working men wore shorter tunics and baggy breeches underneath.

By the end of the Middle Ages noblemen's clothing had become very stylish. Their tunics were cut very short. They wore jackets or jerkins on top. Shoes with very long pointed toes, called 'poulaines' were fashionable. A man's rank was shown by the length of his shoes.

Women, at first, wore loose dresses or kirtles, covered with an over-dress or 'cote-hardie'. By the fourteenth century, dresses were cut very low at the front. The top was laced very tightly to fit the body. Married women always covered their hair and wore various types of veils and head-dresses.

## The Crusades

During the Middle Ages soldiers from all over Europe went off to fight in the Crusades. They brought back the new styles and materials that they found there. Gauze was a fine material from Gaza. Damask was a rich material from Damascus.

## Fashions in the towns

During the fourteenth century the towns became larger. There were more merchants and craftsmen. Tailors began to make a variety of shaped clothes. These were much better fitting with many stitched seams and pleats.

Young men began to wear very short tunics that showed off their legs. Noble women wore such long dresses that the material was gathered at the front.

Many church leaders disliked these new styles. They thought that the men's tunics were indecent. They believed that the Devil danced on the long trains of the women's dresses. The laced fronts of the dresses were called 'Hell's windows'.

Serfs were very poor. Their clothes were made from coarse materials and were in dull colours.

A parti-coloured' outfit was half in one colour, half in another. Ladies' dresses were often trimmed with fur and jewelled.

Burgundian fashions were very rich and ornamented indeed. They were made out of materials like velvet and silk.

Merchants and their families did not wear such rich clothes as the nobles.

19

# The tailor's art

As tailors grew more skilled at their work, the clothes became more complicated in their design. This boy is wearing a tunic with slashed sleeves and bodice. The coloured lining shows through.

The man is wearing a tight-fitting doublet, a ruff and a short fur-trimmed cloak.

This painting by an artist called Breughel shows a scene at a peasant wedding.

Fashionable women wore very wide skirts with tiny waists.

They wore corsets to make their waists even smaller.

Their skirts were held out by a farthingale.

By the end of the Middle Ages many famous scientists and artists were living and working in Europe. In the sixteenth century people all over Europe began to feel that they were living in a new world of adventure and discovery. This was called the Renaissance, (the Rebirth).

## Padding and slashing

Tailors grew adventurous too. Clothes began to bulge out in stiff, fantastic shapes. Fashionable men wore capes and short, padded tunics. These were called doublets (because they were made from a double thickness of cloth). Men also padded out the top of their hose to make them swell out. They often had slits cut into their clothing to show the different colour of the lining, or of the material underneath. This was called 'slashing'. Both men and women wore slashed clothes.

A simple lace collar was worn at first. Later it grew wider and wider. Both men and women wore these 'ruffs'. Some grew so large that they had to be held out on wire frames.

## Hoops and corsets

Women's costumes changed too. The top of the dress was now separated from the skirt. The top was called the 'body' or bodice. It was worn over tightly fitting 'stays' or corsets. They were made of layers of heavy canvas stiffened with whalebone or even of metal. The metal ones were probably worn by women with back troubles. Kirtles were stiffened with padded rolls called 'bum rolls', or wheel-shaped supports called 'farthingales'.

In the Elizabethan period of the late sixteenth century, fashions for court wear were very extravagant. A great deal of very expensive materials and jewellery was worn.

## In the country

Country and working people wore very simple styles that were often out-of-date. They still made their own clothes. They used linen and woollen fabrics for shirts, jackets and trousers. Sometimes leather was worn too. Their styles changed only very slowly. They were never as exaggerated as those of the wealthy. Men wore their tunics as shirts, tucked inside their breeches. Working women gradually came to wear separate skirts and bodices. The bodice was laced very tightly.

# Puritans and Cavaliers

During the middle of the seventeenth century England was ravaged by a civil war. The King, and his Cavalier supporters, believed that the King alone was the ruler of the country. Those who fought against him were the Parliamentarians and Puritans. They thought that Parliament and the people should have some say in ruling the country.

The different beliefs of the two sides can be seen in their clothes. The Puritans had a strict religion which preached hard work and simple living. They wore plain clothes in greys and browns with plain collars and cuffs of white linen. Men often cut their hair short.

On the other side were the followers of the King. They wore brighter colours and clothes of fine materials with lace collars and ribbons. The Cavalier men liked to wear their hair in long ringlets.

These two styles could be seen in other countries. The hard-working merchants of Holland, for example, wore Puritan clothes. Many of the early settlers in North America were Puritans. In the royal courts of France and Spain, however, Cavalier finery was more fashionable.

## Jackets and wigs

Although the Parliamentarians and Puritans won the civil war and ruled in Britain for a short time, the fashion for Cavalier finery returned when Charles II was king.

At his court there was a fashion for wide-legged petticoat breeches called 'rhinegreaves'. Charles himself started a new fashion in men's wear. In 1666 he began wearing a long coat. It was split down the middle and buttoned. He wore a second coat underneath. In time the inner coat became shorter. It was known as the 'waistcoat'. The outer one became known as a jacket. This was the beginning of the modern three-piece suit.

Another king set a new fashion too. Louis XIV of France had a luxurious wig made when he started to go bald. Others started to copy him. But at first only rich men wore wigs.

Restoration women wore stays and petticoats and an over-dress. This was often draped up at the back and had a long train. It was called a 'mantua' dress.

In the towns and among the wealthy people it was possible to see which side a person supported in the Civil War by the clothes that he or she wore. But in the country clothes changed only very slowly and were not affected by the Civil War. They could not afford the finery worn by the Cavaliers or the good quality clothes worn by the richer Puritans. The poorer people both in the towns and country still wore clothes made out of rough, materials in dull colours.

A Cavalier family

A Puritan couple

During the Civil War the clothes that the opposite sides wore were very different. The Cavaliers wore fine clothes made from rich materials like silk and lace. The Puritans, as they believed in a plain, hard-working life, suited their clothes to this. They wore clothes in dark colours with white linen collars and cuffs.

# Ladies and gentlemen

In the eighteenth century elegant men wore silk coats, waistcoats and knee breeches made of matching silk or wool. The coats had flaring skirts, deep cuffs and pockets. Men wore knitted stockings and buckled shoes. Their wigs were shorter and powdered grey with cornflour. Only the very poorest men wore trousers. When the French Revolution broke out in 1789, noblemen referred to the rioting poor as 'sans-culottes' (those without breeches).

## Ladies

Eighteenth century ladies wore costly silks. The wealthy could afford to change their dresses often. Others had to make them last for years. Ladies wore hoops and padding again. Paniers made the dresses stand out at the sides. Later women wore a cork 'rump' which made the dress stand out at the back instead.

Ladies wore false hair pieces. They wired and pow-

dered their hair into very fancy styles. They decorated these hairstyles with feathers, bows and even little scenes with people, animals or ships.

Ordinary women had to think of ways of getting similar effects. Some girls made their own hoops with slender canes. A cushion or a roll of padding would serve as a rump or panier.

## Dandies

There have always been men who are particularly noted for their outrageous clothes. In 1764 a group of fashionable playboys set up a club called the Macaroni Club. They wore exaggerated styles with lots of false hair, fancy lace and tight sleeves. Fashionable young men became known as Macaronis or dandies. When an English writer wanted to poke fun at American troops, he wrote the famous song:

> Yankee Doodle came to town
> Riding on a pony
> Stuck a feather in his cap
> and called it Macaroni.

French dandies developed their own styles after the Revolution. They were known as Incroyables (Incredibles).

Above: Hedgehog wig. Some ladies wore wigs too.

Above left: A group of young men formed the Macaroni Club in the early 1770's. They wore clothes that most people thought were outrageous. They wore wigs that were high off their foreheads. The wigs were powdered, and tied with velvet or satin ribbons.

Left: This painting by William Hogarth shows some of the fashionable people of the eighteenth century.

Right: A laundry maid at work is shown in this painting by Morland.

# Buying and selling

Before the coming of machines and factories, there were fewer goods for sale. Most people lived in the country. From the Middle Ages to the end of the eighteenth century most buying and selling was done at weekly village markets. Bigger fairs were held once a year. People came from miles around to go to the fair.

Weavers brought their cloth to the fairs and markets and people bought it to make their own clothes at home. People could also buy clothes such as shoes that were more difficult to make. They might also be able to afford small trinkets, such as pins, brooches, buckles and ribbons.

### In the towns

There were larger covered markets in the towns. Here craftsmen of the Middle Ages sold their goods in booths and stalls. They also sold their goods in their own workshops. These workshops seldom had windows. Through the open doors you could see the tailor or cobbler at work.

By the time of the Renaissance, merchants had come to play a more important part in buying and selling.

A street scene in a medieval town looked very different from a modern high street. The shops were much smaller and the craftsmen often worked in them. Pedlars were in the street selling their goods too.

Ladies choose their materials in a nineteenth century draper's shop.

Sometimes they lent the craftsman money to set up his workshop. They brought the raw materials to the weaver and took away the finished cloth. They sold the cloth to the tailors.

Rich merchants dealt in materials from abroad. Others travelled between the towns and the country. They went on horseback or mule. Poorer pedlars travelled on foot.

## Shops

By the early nineteenth century fewer craftsmen sold their goods directly to the public in their own workshops. There were now special shops where buying and selling was done. Shopkeeping became a trade of its own. Few people still made all the clothes they wore. As more and more people moved from the country to work in the factories in the towns, they did not have time to make their own clothes any more.

'Open shops' were simple trestle tables set up in the street. 'Standing shops' were houses whose front rooms were used for buying and selling. In fashionable parts of the big cities, these standing shops had glass-fronted windows. People could see a great variety of goods laid out for display inside.

# The machine age

Two great revolutions happened in the eighteenth century. One was the French Revolution. It brought new ideas of justice and equality. The other was a revolution in making goods, called the Industrial Revolution. It brought machines and factories.

In 1733 John Kay built a 'flying shuttle' which made the weaving of cloth much quicker. In 1767 James Hargreaves invented a 'spinning jenny' which could spin several threads at the same time. Later, machines were driven by water and steam power. These produced thread and cloth at a very fast rate.

Cloth manufacturers built huge factories to house the new machinery. Many country people flocked to work in the new factories. New 'factory towns' grew up.

## Effects

The factory towns became prosperous for the owners and merchants. The men, women and children who worked

A young matchseller. Poor people could not always afford shoes.

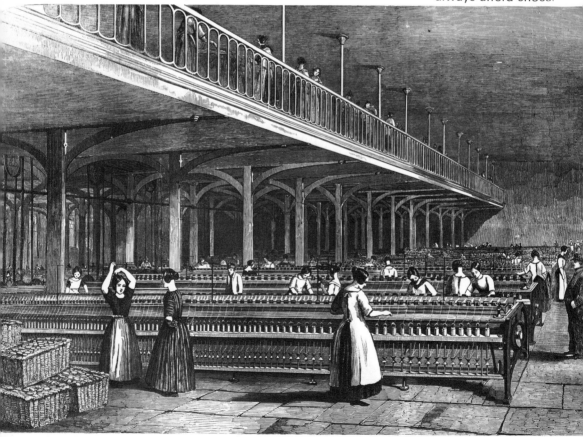

Children on the way to work in the mills.

Left: Girls at work in the textile factories.

Below: Men at work making machinery for the new factories.

Right: Many clothes were made in 'sweat shops'. The people that worked in these were very poor and worked long hours.

in the factories mostly lived in slum houses. They were very poor. They never bought new clothes. They had to go to rag fairs and cheap market stalls to buy their clothes. These were often third, fourth or fifth hand. The filthy rags helped to spread disease in the industrial towns.

## The clothing of the poor

Amongst the slightly better off there was a growing demand for cheap but stylish clothes. These were bought by people who could not afford better quality clothes. They wanted to look smarter than they could really afford. By the 1840's there was a big sale in this type of clothing. Cheap ready-to-wear clothes were made by tailors and needlewomen in poorer districts of the larger towns. They worked at home or in dark and stuffy 'sweat shops'. They were amongst the poorest workers and hardly earned enough to feed their children.

A journalist called Henry Mayhew went to interview some needlewomen. He found that they were dressed in the most thin and miserable rags. When he asked if these were their only clothes, they laughed bitterly. They did not even own the rags. They had borrowed their tattered shawls and petticoats to look smart for the interview.

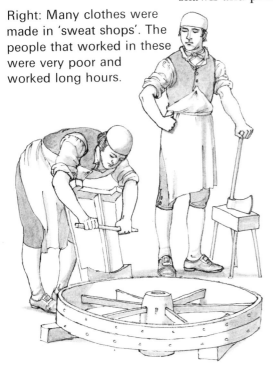

# Working clothes

One effect of the French Revolution was to make full-length trousers fashionable. At first they were thought 'revolutionary' and not respectable. The English dandy, Beau Brummel, began to wear trousers in the early years of the nineteenth century. They soon caught on among men of fashion. By the 1820's, however, they had been accepted and were worn by nearly all men. Countrymen were less interested in following fashion. They kept their old-fashioned knee breeches and wore them for many more years.

With full-length trousers, jackets and waistcoats the modern three-piece suit had come into being. At first the three different parts were worn in three different colours. Jackets were cut back to show bright waistcoats underneath. But as the years passed the colours came to match each other. They also grew darker and darker. Bright colours were worn only by women. Men came to think that it was not suitable for them to wear bright clothes. Only tweed suits for country wear showed much variety.

By the nineteenth century the three-piece suit looked very much as it does today.

## Regional costume

Poor people working in the towns could not afford finery. They did not even have the time to spare from their work to weave and make their own clothes. In country areas, however, the people still made their own clothes. They wore their own simple country or peasant styles. These varied from village to village. They were based on very old styles and did not change like fashionable clothes.

By the end of the nineteenth century peasants began to buy dyes, embroidery threads, ribbons and materials in the country town markets. Pedlars took these things to the villages. Gradually peasant dress changed. It became more colourful and fancy. Young people moved to the towns to find work in the factories. They began to wear town styles. Slowly peasant dress went out of everyday use. It is usually only worn for special occasions now. Many different countries have their own style of peasant dress. It has influenced fashion all over the world in recent years. South American ponchos and Indian kaftans are popular in many big cities today, for example.

cabdriver

the country and for sports en wore a tweed suit. It as not as formal as the ree-piece suit.

This print shows Hyde Park as it was in the nineteenth century. You can see many of the clothes that we have talked about.

These are some of the uniforms and special working clothes worn in the nineteenth century.

navvy

postman

policeman

fireman

# Clothes for women

crinoline

bustle

corset

So that they could be fashionable women wore many different sorts of hoops, frames and corsets. Here are some of them.

The people who made the French Revolution admired the way of life of the ancient Greeks and Romans. Later, fashionable people wanted to copy classical clothes. Of course, they did not wear tunics and togas, but they aimed for simple flowing lines. In the early years of the nineteenth century, French women started to wear white, high-waisted Greek dresses with long trains. Most women could afford to wear these dresses as they were made out of a cheap material called cotton muslin. Rich women wore the dresses with expensive shawls made in brightly woven colours.

## Crinolines and bustles

In the middle of the nineteenth century tight corsets and full skirts came back into fashion. Up to 12 petticoats were worn to hold the skirts out. Then hooped cages made of flexible steel were invented. These were worn instead of all the petticoats. Almost every girl that could afford the money wore a crinoline.

Crinolines could fly up in the wind. Women wore knickerbockers or 'drawers' underneath. These underclothes were some of the first type of knickers.

By the 1870's women began to wear 'bustles' instead of crinolines. These were frames or padded cushions that stuck out at the back, but not all the way round the figure.

## The new woman

Many women worked in factories like men, others wanted to train for jobs as doctors and lawyers. Few women were allowed to do these jobs. They were not allowed to vote or own their own homes, and were treated as though they were inferior to men. Many women did not like the huge steel cages and fashionable clothes that they were expected to wear. They wanted to wear sensible clothes which would give them greater freedom of movement. These women were called the 'New Women'.

Some of the new women joined the Dress Reform movement. They refused to wear corsets or very fashionable clothes. Instead they wore 'rationals' or 'sensible' dress. This was usually a plain shirt, jacket and flared or divided skirt.

Above left: A classical style dress with a high waistline.

Above centre: Many crinolines were so full that it was difficult to walk around furniture and through doors.

Above right: After the crinoline the bustle became **fashionable**. Frames were worn to make the back of the skirt stick out.

Right: Towards the end of the nineteenth century women began to wear more sensible clothes. They were called 'rationals'. The women could move around in them more easily.

Far right: When cycling became popular some women found their full skirts very difficult to manage. They began to wear bloomers for cycling.

33

# New freedoms

After the horrors of World War I everyone hoped for a better and happier life. However, many people were out of work. For them life was very hard. They had to struggle to find enough money for food and certainly could not afford smart clothes.

The richer, young people seemed to turn their backs on all this hardship. They were determined to have a good time. The girls shocked their elders by the clothes they wore. They cut their hair short and wore knee-length skirts for the first time in history. They wore make-up and smoked cigarettes in public. They were called the 'Flappers' or 'Bright Young Things'. In the 1930's skirts grew longer. Evening dresses were often backless.

## Sports dress

Men still wore three-piece suits, but casual and sports dress became common too. Hiking, rambling and cycling were popular with everyone in the 1930's. Young people wore shorts and open-necked shirts. Women wore trousers in the country, but not yet in the towns. As women took more part in sports people gradually became used to seeing more of the body than they had for centuries.

The flappers of the 1920's often wore short skirts with fringes.

The swimming suit has changed a great deal since the beginning of the century
Far left: Edwardian bathing costume
Left: 1930's swimming suit
Below: 1970's swimming s

## Making do

World War II had a big effect on fashion. In many countries it was thought vulgar to wear expensive clothes. Cloth was in short supply. In Britain, the government ordered special designs for 'utility' clothes from famous dress designers. They were practical, smart and used as little material as possible. Clothes were rationed and everyone became used to making do. Cheap and sensible fabrics were used. Knitting wool was re-used. Clothes were made from curtains, parachute silk, dusters and even old silk wall maps. Women wore headscarves instead of hats. They wore trousers for everyday life.

The war also brought changes in men's clothes. Woollen roll-neck sweaters and hooded duffle coats kept seamen warm in cold weather. Airmen wore leather jackets. After the war these clothes were adapted for leisure wear.

Above left: Women became used to wearing trousers for work during World War II. Here are some women working in the fields. They were called land girls.

Below: Clothes worn for leisure time and for sports have changed a lot. Here are a fisherman in 1910, a golfer in 1930 and a modern man wearing jeans and a casual jacket.

# The great fashion houses

Fashionable people have always wanted to keep up with the latest styles. In the early days most fashions started in the royal courts. Nobles who lived in the country had to write to their friends at court to find out what the people were wearing.

Some noble women had special fashion dolls made. These dolls were dressed in the latest fashions and sent all over Europe.

By the end of the eighteenth century printers began to sell fashion pictures. The best ones came from Paris, the centre of the fashion world. Gossip magazines began to include these pictures. By the early 1800's special fashion magazines started up. These printed pictures of all the latest Paris fashions.

1910

These silhouettes show how hemlines and shapes have changed since the beginning of the century.

## Fashion sensations

Bit by bit a fashion industry came into being. Fashion designers began to create fashions. The best designers kept their 'creations' secret until the last minute. They sold the designs for a lot of money. They hired other designers to work for them and set up fashion houses.

Fashion became big business. The designers created new fashions regularly. There were fashions for spring, summer, autumn and winter.

## Fashion houses

Sometimes the designers caused sensations. After World War II women had got used to cheap, sensible clothes. A French designer called Christian Dior invented the 'New Look'. This brought back long, full skirts and shaped jackets that were nipped in at the waist. Many people were scandalized. They thought the New Look was much too luxurious.

Another fashion sensation happened in the 1960's. Women had become used to skirts being quite long. When the mini-skirt was brought out it was thought indecent to show so much leg.

As young people came to wear what they liked, the fashion houses became less important. Many new fashions are started by younger designers working for smaller boutiques and ready-to-wear firms. The large clothing companies copy these designs.

Below: A fashion show of the 1920's in Paris.

1920's     1930's     1940's     1960's

Right: Mary Quant, one of the most famous designers of the 1960's, made the mini-skirt very popular. This fashion sketch shows some different designs.

Below right: This model is wearing the 'New Look'. After the hardship of World War II it was thought very luxurious.

Below left: War-time utility clothes designed by Norman Hartnell.

# Young fashions

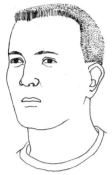

Crewcut

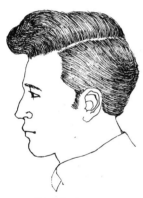

Teddy boy

Hair today

Men's hairstyles have changed quite a lot over the last thirty years.

The idea of special fashions for young people is quite new. After World War II, wages were higher and younger people had more money to spend. These 'teenagers' began to develop their own tastes in music and clothes.

Some teenagers just went on wearing comfortable children's clothes such as jeans and sweaters. Others spent their money on new styles of their own. In the 1950's, for example, young men began to copy styles of the Edwardian Age (at the beginning of this century). They wore tight 'drain-pipe' trousers, long drape jackets, embroidered waistcoats and brightly coloured socks. They were called 'Teddy Boys'.

Teenage hairstyles became quite different from adult ones. Teddy boys slicked back their hair in long, greasy quiffs. The spiky 'crew-cut' was another popular style. In the 1960's, boys began to grow their hair very long. Older people thought that this was ridiculous. But if you look back through this book, you can see that men have often worn their hair long.

## Entertainers

Entertainers have always been great trend-setters. Hundreds of years ago, actors and actresses were among the few people who set fashions outside the royal courts. From the 1920's and 1930's, people all over the world followed the styles set by film stars. Teenagers might not copy their parents, or the great fashion designers, but they often took ideas from films, television and pop stars.

## Styles from abroad

More than anything else young people stopped obeying rules and regulations about what they should wear. They wore what they liked and what was comfortable. Over the last ten years there has been an interest in peasant or 'ethnic clothes'. These come from all over the world. Some are original, but many more are copied here. People seem to want special hand-made clothes again. Perhaps they no longer think that mass-produced clothes are best. People still make their own clothes as they have done for hundreds of years. If you make clothes at home you can make sure that they fit properly and have just the style you want.

# Protective clothes

Shaping metal is almost as old a craft as weaving. Since the earliest days, fighting men have worn armour to protect their heads and bodies from enemy blows.

The shape of the armour often changed when clothes were cut in a new way. The armour of the early Middle Ages, for example, hung in loose lengths of chain mail like tunics and kirtles of woven cloth. Later, clothes became more fitted and stitched. Armour was made in sections and panels too.

Although armour gave protection, it was also used for display. Nobles spent fortunes on it. They inlaid their armour with precious metals.

Armour often became more trouble than it was worth. Crusaders baked inside their metal suits. A French knight at the Battle of Agincourt complained that his armour was so heavy that he could only move very slowly. He had to keep stopping to catch his breath.

Armour was no protection against gunpowder and cannon balls. Body armour gradually disappeared, though soldiers still wear helmets today.

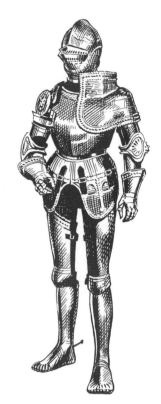

Above: This suit of armour was worn by Henry VIII. It was inlaid with metals to form patterns. Rich men liked their suits of armour to be as fashionable as their everyday clothes.

Left: This ratcatcher is wearing a fantail hat to protect his head and a leather mitt to protect his hand.

Below: Special shoes are worn to protect feet.

## Protection at work

The apron is one of the oldest pieces of protective clothing. Both men and women wore aprons in the Middle Ages. Craftsmen came to wear aprons whose colour showed what their trade was. In the nineteenth century, butchers wore aprons with stripes that ran from side to side. Fishmongers wore aprons with stripes that ran from top to bottom. Barbers wore check aprons.

Nowadays, workmen usually wear overalls. For housework and for working in shops, women often wear house coats instead of aprons.

## Rainwear

In the early nineteenth century, a man called Charles Mackintosh invented coats that were treated with rubber to make them waterproof. These early 'mackintoshes' gave off a terrible smell. Since then, people have found much better ways of making rainwear. They use materials called synthetics that are made from chemicals. Synthetic materials are now used for many different things. Many clothes are made from them and many things around the house, in fact all round us.

Above: Butchers have traditionally worn aprons with blue and white stripes running across them.

Right: Rainwear is a form of protective clothing. It protects us from the rain.

Below: Miners at work wear safety helmets.

# Making clothes today

The Industrial Revolution brought new ways of making goods quickly and cheaply. It also brought new ways of buying and selling. In the middle of the nineteenth century people began to sell clothes in great stores. These had different departments. You could buy a hat, a suit or a pair of shoes all in the same building.

Some of these stores like Harrods and Dickens and Jones in London were very grand and elegant. Others sold cheaper clothes.

A man called William Whitely set up a store called the Universal Provider. He printed a catalogue showing all the goods he had for sale and sent these to his customers. People could order their clothes from their own homes. Delivery vans took his goods all over the country. Now many stores do this.

Today self-service shops and shopping centres have made buying and selling even easier. In the 1960's smaller boutiques (shops) grew up in most towns. They sold more original and special clothes. In most big cities today you can still see people with small street-market stalls. They still sell all sorts of new and second-hand

Clothes are sold in many different places from small shops and boutiques to large department stores. You can also buy clothes in many markets.

Above left: Inside a modern department store.

Above right: A modern market.

Many clothes from baby wear to evening dresses, protective clothes and sportswear are made from synthetic materials. How many of your clothes are made from synthetic fibres?

clothes and trinkets, just like the pedlars of hundreds of years ago.

## New materials

For thousands of years people used only natural materials such as wool, cotton, flax, silk and leather. In the twentieth century people found new ways of making materials from chemicals. The first of these materials was artificial silk, or rayon. It came into use after 1910. Nylon came into use just before World War II. Other fabrics such as Orlon, Terylene and PVC soon followed. They are called synthetic materials.

Synthetic materials can be stretched and moulded. They are used to make nearly everything nowadays, from men's suits and expensive evening dresses to the latest lightweight underwear.

Synthetic materials are cheap to make in large quantities. They can be dyed so that the colours never run. We have not yet seen all of their possibilities. We can only guess what influence they will have on the clothes that people will wear a hundred years from now.

As natural materials became more scarce, we will have to rely more and more on synthetic fibres. Many synthetic materials that we use today are made from crude oil. As the oil that we have discovered runs out we will have to find new ways of making the materials that we need. The synthetic materials of the future may be very different from those we use now.

43

## Books to read

Muffs and morals, Binder; Harrap 1953

Body and clothes, Broby-Johansen; Faber & Faber 1968

Occupational costume, Cunnington and Lucas; Black 1967

The wearing of costume, Green; Pitman 1966

Costume cavalcade, Hansen; Eyre Methuen 1976

People and shopping, Harrison; Ernest Benn 1975

Ancient Greek, Roman and Byzantine costume, Houston; Black 1947

Ancient Egyptian, Mesopotamian and Persian Costume; Black 1954

A concise history of costume, Laver; Thames and Hudson 1969

Costumes of everyday life, Lister; Barrie and Jenkins 1972

Rural costume, Oaks and Hamilton Hill; Batsford 1970

Antique paper dolls 1919–1920, Arnold; Dover 1975

Fashion from Ancient Egypt to the present day, Contini; Hamlyn 1965

Look at clothes, Binder; Hamish Hamilton 1963

Starters Long Ago: Clothes and Costume; Weapons and Armour; Macdonald Educational

Visual Books: Fashion and Clothes; Arms and Armour; Macdonald Educational

## Places to visit

Many museums have displays of costume through the ages. Here are some of them. Your local library might be able to help you too.

London: Victoria and Albert Museum, Bethnal Green Museum, Museum of Mankind, Museum of the City of London, Horniman Museum.

Brighton: Brighton Art Gallery and Museum.

Worthing: Museum and Art Gallery.

Birmingham: Museum and Art Gallery.

Leicester: Wygston's House.

York: Castle Museum, the Gallery of Costume at Castle Howard.

Worcester: costume collection at Hartlebury Castle.

Norwich: Strangers' Hall Museum of Domestic Life.

Manchester: Gallery of Costume at Platt Hall.

Bath: Museum of Costume, Assembly Rooms.

Edinburgh: Royal Scottish Museum, National Museum of Antiquities of Scotland.

Bristol: costume collection at Blaise Castle Folk Museum.

Cardiff: Welsh Folk Museum.

# Index

Where an illustration appears
as well as a mention in the text
the page number is **bold**.

Apron **41**
Armour **40**

Barbette **18**
Belts 14, 16
Bloomers **33**
Bodice 21
Boutiques 42
Breeches 12, 16, 18, **19**, 22, **24**, 30
Bum rolls 21
'Bright Young Things' 34
Bustle **32, 33**

Camel hair 16
Capes 12, 21
Cavaliers 22, **23**
Charms 6
Chiton **14**
Cloaks **16, 17, 20**
Coats **24**, 35
Collar 21, 22, **23**
Corsets 9, **11, 21, 32**
Cote-hardie 18, **19**
Cotton 6, 43
Cotton muslin 32
Crinoline **32, 33**
Crispine **18**
Cuffs 22, **23**, 24

Damask 18
Dandies **24**, 25
Department stores **42**
Display 8
Distaff **13**
Doublet **20**, 21
Draping 6, **12, 14, 15**
Drawers 32
Dresses 12, 16, **17**, 18, **19**, 22
Duffle coats 35
Dyes 12, 18, 30, 43

Embroidery 12, 16, 18, 30, 38
Ethnic clothes **38**

Factories **28**
Fairs 26, 29
Fantail hat **40**
Farthingale **21**
Fashion 8, **36, 37**
Fashion dolls 36
Feet 9
Felt 16
Fillet **18**
Flappers **34**
Flax 6, 12, 43
Flying shuttle 28

Gauze 18
Girdles 16

Hairstyles **15**, 21, **25**, 34, **38**
Hats 35, 40
Head-dresses **18**
Headscarves 35
Helmet **41**
Himation **14**
Hoops 9, 24
Hose 18, **19**

Jackets 14, **15**, 18, **19**, 21, 22, **30**, 31, 32, **33**, 38
Jeans **35**, 38
Jerkins 18, **19**
Jewellery 8, **16**, 21

Kilts 12
Kirtle 18, **19**, 21
Knickerbockers 32
Knickers 32

Lace 21
Leather 12, 15, 16, 18, 21, 43

Legs 9
Linen 15, 16, 18, 21, 22
Loincloth 12
Loom 12, **13**

Magic 6
Make-up **8**, 9
Markets 26, 29, 42, **43**
Mini-skirt 36, **37**
Mitts **40**

'New Look' **36**
'New Woman' 32

Overalls 41

Paniers 24
Peasant dress 30
Peplos **14**
Petticoats 22, 32
Plus-fours **35**
Pockets 24
Poulaines **10**, 18, **19**
Primitive people 6, **7**
Puritans 22, **23**

Rag fairs 29
Rainwear **41**
'Rationals' 32
Rhinegreaves 22
Ruff **20, 21**
Rump 24
Sans-culottes 24
Sewing 6, 12
Shawls 32, **33**
Shirts 16, **17**, 21, 32, **33**, 34
Shoes **10**, 18, **19, 24**, 26
Shops 27, 42
Shorts 34
Silk 6, 12, 15, 16, 18, 24, 35, 43
Skins 6

Skirts 9, 14, **15,** 24, 32, **33,** 34
Slashing **20,** 21
Spindle 12, **13**
Socks 38
Spinning 6
Spinning jenny 28
Spinning wheel **13**
Stays 21, 22
Stockings **24**
Stolas 15
Suit 22, **30, 31,** 34, **35**
Sumptuary laws 10
Sweat shops **29**
Sweaters 35, 38
Swimming suits **34**
Synthetics 41, 43

Toga **14,** 15
Trousers 6, 12, 15, 21, 24, **30, 31,** 34, **35,** 38
Tunics 12, **14, 15, 16,** 18
Tweed 30, **31, 35**

Uniforms 10, **11, 31**
'Utility' clothes 35, **37**

Veils **18**

Waistcoat 22, **24, 30, 31,** 38
Waists 9, 14, 32
Weavers 26
Weaving 6, 12, 28
Wigs 10, 22, 24, **25**

Wool 6, 12, 15, 16, 18, 21, 2
35, 43
Workshops 26

Yak hair 16

Zoccolos **9**